How to Outline a Nonfiction Book

Copyright 2017
Dean R. Giles

Thank you valued customer for your purchase. We have a
valuable gift for you

Free Adult Stress Relief Coloring Book
FreeColoringBook.Org/gift

Claim your gift at

Contents

Chapter 1 – Introduction

Are you struggling to start your nonfiction book? Are you looking for a way to easily and clearly organize so that you can get your writing off to a great start? So many people know that they can write a nonfiction book. They have the knowledge that can be shared— and there are so many people out there that need the knowledge that they have to share! But the book hasn't been written because getting started is so overwhelming.

Many writers find that the writing is the easy part. The harder part is getting the outline down so that they have a map to follow with the writing. If you have been struggling to start your book, this is the resource that you need. Not only will you get great instructions on how to make an outline, but you will get good advice on how to start you book, where to go for the little bit of research that will make your book pop, plenty of examples of great outlines, and 10 ready to use outline templates. There is a template for 10 different types of nonfiction books. No matter what type of nonfiction book you want to write—there is a template here for you.

What is an Outline?

An outline can be the map to your writing success. It can be your guide to your final destination. If you do it right, an outline can create a table of contents. An outline can be a tool that will prevent you from doing a lot of rewriting and reorganizing.

Let me explain it with this example. If you were dumped, with your car, onto some random street in Huston Texas and told to meet someone at Richmond and Weslayan, you might be able to find that intersection by asking people on the street. You might get there by following traffic, or by sheer dumb luck.

But, I would suspect that you would get there faster with a map, and maybe even faster with a GPS or a service like Google Maps giving you directions from your smart phone. The take away here is that it is much harder to reach a specific destination without some guide showing you how to get there, especially when you have never been there before.

Given enough time and unlimited resources, you will get to your destination eventually—but it won't be in a straight line. It may cost a lot in gas and time. But having a guide will help you get there in the least amount of time with the fewest detours.

That is what an outline for a book is all

about. It isn't set in stone, and shouldn't be applied like a straight-jacket, it is simply a guide that will keep centering you on the path to the end of your book, it will kill idle time, stop endless rewrites, and help you avoid writer's block.

Best of all, an outline gives you a chance to see the entire project from a whole view perspective. This perspective will keep reminding you of your destination and why you want to get there. Have you ever been interrupted in the middle of a thought, then found that you couldn't remember what you were saying before the interruption?

An outline can be a gentle nudge back to what is important, and it can give you the motivation to finish the project — because you can see the end, and on paper, that end isn't that far away!

Example of a Nonfiction Book Outline

Short Experience Based Book

Title: Re-Entering the Job Market
I. I Never Saw It Coming
    1. Getting Laid-Off Sucks
    2. Why Didn't I Network in the Past?
    3. No One Understands
II. Starting from Scratch
    1. Taking Inventory

Notice that I used the standard Roman Numeral Outline Format that you learned back in grade school. It is a good format for an outline, but as a book outline, this format really doesn't help you that much.

For every outline going forward, I have tried to make the outlines more like a table of contents. That is your end goal.

Write the table of contents first — then you will know exactly what you will put into your book. With a good table-of-contents outline, you may be able to just add the words and you will have a book.

So be prepared for outlines that look and

read more like books, and notice that many examples are pulled right from the table of contents of real books!

Why Outline?

There is a big debate that is ongoing. What is best? Using an outline or just sitting down to write "by the seat of your pant." The debate is usually over fiction books, and has more to do with allowing the story to be told by the characters, and letting the inspiration of the moment be your writing muse.

There are famous people that use both methods: Orson Scott Card and Brandon Sanderson are writers that believe in outlines. Stephen King does not. I like to straddle the two methods. I like to start with a great outline, then modify it or leave out parts of the outline completely as the book begins to take on some of its own characteristics. I believe strongly in a great outline, but I never let the outline interrupt the creativity of the moment, or force me into poor decisions.

Outlines have helped me a lot in the past. The exercises in creating an outline have borne fruit again and again for me. I have found topics, subtopics, issues, and other things to address that I would never have found without going through the process of creating an outline.

Sam Oliver, in his book "Another Path into Healing", talked about how writing was one of his healing methods, and that after he had a title and a table of contents created, his book would almost write itself. I have found that to be the case. Once I have the outline, the rest flows together very smoothly, and I can write by using the outline as a reference and a framework.

The Outline as a Window into the Soul of Your Book

There is an old saying, don't judge a book by its cover—but we often do. We often must judge a book by its cover, because there are so many books and so little time. Once a potential customer has decided that they like your cover, and your title, then has been interested by the blurb that accompanies the cover and title, the potential customer may then look at the table of contents.

The table of contents is the outline of your book—it gives a potential reader a chance to peer into the essence of the book. If the table of contents doesn't look inviting and doesn't grab the potential customer's interest immediately — then it is likely that you have lost the sale, and the book won't be read. The outline is what maps the flow of your book, the magic of your book will start right here with an outline.

A Stitch in Time Saves Nine

The subheading above is an old saying that eludes to fixing a tear in fabric. If you make a stitch when you see the tear just beginning, you may save yourself nine stitches later. The gist of the saying is that doing things at the right time, and specifically early in the process, can save a BUNDLE of work on the back end. Writing is hard enough as it is! You don't want to backtrack and rewrite again and again. One of the big benefits of outlining is that you cut down on the backtracking and the rewriting. Do the outline and see how it speeds up your writing.

Using This Book

This book was meant to be a reference book. It was designed to be somewhat modular. As you look at the table of contents, if you see areas that you think that you understand well, you can skip those chapters and dig right into what you picked up this book to learn.

I would still suggest reading the entire book, then going back to reread the sections that you might need a little help with, because you never know what gem you might pick up. There is a quote from the movie "Inception" that I like a lot: "A single idea from the human mind can build cities.

An idea can transform the world and rewrite all the rules." One idea can change everything! I have tried to assemble many ideas and concepts that I hope will be a springboard to your own imagination and will grow into ideas of your own and methods of your own that will far surpass anything that you read here! Also look for ways to apply what you read. All of the knowledge in the world does you very little good if you fail to implement any of it.

Conclusion

Writing is faster, more direct, can be more organized, and flow better if it is approached with an outline. The outline can be formatted to create a Table of Contents for your book. The outline can be used as the map that gets you from the beginning and doesn't let you down until you get to the end of your book.

There are so many ways to use an outline, and so many things an outline can do for your writing. The biggest problem with an outline is that it has to be elastic, it can't be used like a straight-jacket to limit your writing, only as a guide post to bring you back to the path that you designed and to keep you from getting lost or unanchored.

Exercises

My father always said the hardest part of any job was just deciding that you were going to do it. The second hardest was just deciding that you wouldn't quit until it was finished. Take the plunge and do the hardest part of this outlining stuff. Decide right now that you will give outlining a real chance.

Choose to start today. Write it down or say it in front of a mirror: "I will start my book by beginning an outline today." Do yourself a favor. Stop reading, and take the book outline challenge. Make up your mind to start your book outline today!

Chapter 2 – Where to Begin

"The hardest part of any journey is taking the first step." By Anonymous

You have some ideas, you want to write a book, but you don't know where to start. Well, welcome to the club. Every writer struggles with starting a book. The topic, the angle, the purpose, the target readers are all things that you need to think about. What you choose for those few variables will largely determine the voice and temperament of your book. But how do you choose those things? How do you know what to write about?

You Have a Story and it is Wonderful

"Everyone has a book inside of them." Jodi

Picoult

You are no different, you do have a book inside of you. You probably have many books inside of you because there are many aspects to your life.

Look at the roles that you play as a Father or Mother, Son or Daughter. Look at the skills that you have as an employee or a service provider. Look at the hobbies that you enjoy. Look at the stories you know about your own life or about the lives of others that you have come in contact with. Look at the treasured tales of your parents or other ancestors. There is so much that you have to share, and so many people who's lives could be enhanced by hearing your stories.

You may have stories about what you have done in life or about what you have learned in life. That type of a book is called a "journey" book, and is a very popular type of book. You have undertaken many journeys in your life, as you started school, as you began your hobbies or your career, as you started dating, or at your first kiss.

There are so many journeys to talk or write about. Below is an example of the outline of a journey book.
It is from the "Foreign Languages for Everyone" by Irene Brouwer Konyndyk
(https://www.amazon.com/Foreign-Languages-

Everyone-Students-Disabilities-ebook/dp/B0071V0SVM).

The subtitle is "How I Learned to Teach Second Languages to Students with Learning Disabilities." It is the account of the learning journey that the author took as she tried and failed, tried and failed, then finally succeeded at something that was important to her. (Shown in the figure below). You have many similar stories from your life. Your experiences could be helpful to many other people. A nonfiction book is a way to share those stories and impart needed advice and help to many people.

Table of Contents

Figure 1, Example Outline of a Learning Journey
type of Book

You Have Advice and Knowledge to Share, and it is Brilliant

What can you do that other people would love to learn? What is your expertise at work? What are you the "go to" person for at work or in the community? What skills have you spent years developing? What skills did you learn from school or from a trade? What can you do better than other people? What difficult problems in your life have you solved? How do you deal with life's difficult situations, such as depression, anxiety, stress, balancing responsibility, or even balancing your check book?

You have so much that you can share! There are people out there that need the knowledge and advice that you have to give. Will you write the book that will change their lives? Will you share a portion of your knowledge that someone else desperately needs?

Selecting What to Write About

There are three things that come together that can make a great book, and by selecting the intersection of the three, you have the best chance of writing a book that will have an impact on others, and might even sell well.

Those three things are: 1) What you know. 2) What you like (are passionate about). 3) What is popular. The intersecting of these three is seen visually in the figure below.

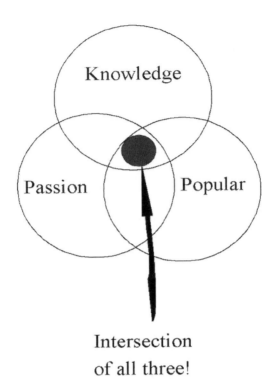

Intersection
of all three!

Figure 2, Intersection of Your Knowledge, Your
Passion, and What's Popular

Notice how a central bullseye can be
carved out of the intersection. That is your
target. The intersection of the three. However,
you can write a successful book in just one of
those quadrants. For example: You can choose to
write solely about something that you know a
lot about. I call those types of book Knowledge

Books. Those types of books are usually very informative and can be the very easy books to write, because they come only from the knowledge already in your head.

However, if the subject is not something that you are passionate about, then the book will probably plod along. And, if the topic is not popular, you may not sell many books. Do you see how the best books need to come from an intersection of those three components — What you know, what you are passionate about, and what is popular.

Example of an Outline for a Knowledge Type Book

Snippet from the Table of Contents of the book "Pure Soapmaking" by Anee-Marie Faiola.

Introduction: The Beauty of Pure, Handmade Soap →

Chapter 1: The Soapmaking Process →

Chapter 2: Choosing Equipment & Molds →

Chapter 3: Step-by-Step Cold-Process Soapmaking →

Chapter 4: All about Oils →

Chapter 5: Using Herbs & Other Natural Additives →

Chapter 6: Scenting Your Soap →

Chapter 7: Designing Recipes →

Chapter 8: All about Simplicity — Recipes →

Figure 3, Example of an Outline of a Knowledge Type Book

Above is an example of an outline of a knowledge type book. It could also be a book that is written with passion and perhaps it is popular. So, the above figure could be a very good example of a good book outline.

What are you passionate about? What do you obsess about? What do you really like, and would love to share it with others. Those thing that appeal to you, that you like, that you want to share are your passions.

When you write about the things that you are passionate about, the writing comes so easily. These are the topics that you are excited about and that you could talk about for hours. When you are passionate about something, you have to tell the world! That enthusiasm is contagious and people can see that you love the topic.

That can make the book interesting, something that people have a hard time putting down, because they can relate to the enthusiasm of the author. In the figure below is an outline of a "Passion" type book. It is called "Skiing is my Passion" by Tommy Waltner, https://www.amazon.com/Skiing-My-Passion-Tommy-Waltner-ebook/dp/B01NCLF63T . Think about the passions in your life.

Contents

Figure 4, Partial Outline of a Passion Type Book
The Big Picture

You also have to decide what you want to get out of your book. Are you writing a book to 1) make money, 2) promote a business, 3) establish your name and reputation, or maybe 4) just to try your hand at writing a book? Knowing why you want to write a book may make a big difference in how you approach it.

If you are wanting a book to establish yourself as an expert in an industry, or if you are just wanting to write a book for the experience, then perhaps your topic is already chosen for you. Choosing a title and an approach aren't as critical, as they might be if what you want to do is sell your book. If you want to sell your book, then the rest of this chapter is dedicated to helping you choose a topic that would have a better chance of selling.

If You Write It, They May Not Come

In the movie "Field of Dreams", Ray Kinsella is convinced that if he builds it, they will come.

If you are writing a book that you will self-publish, then you need to realize that self-publishing opened the world to many more writers than it had in the past—however, in the past, publishing companies did a lot of the heavy lifting of getting the book out and advertising it.

In the book "APE, Author, Publisher, Entrepreneur", Guy Kawaski and Shawn Welch, explained that today's author has to dabble in publishing and entrepreneurship to get his book out there. Does that mean that you have to spend the rest of your life pitching or selling your book? No! But designing your book correctly for publishing and sales can do amazing things when it comes to marketing the book. Amazon will help you sell your book if you design the sales features correctly.

There are entire books and courses written that cover lots and lots of these variables and considerations. I'm only going to mention a few of the most important ones. If you get these few things right you will make sales. If you don't get these few things right, you may not sell a single book. You have to decide now.
If you are interested in preparing your book for sales, then you will want to pay close attention to the rest of this chapter.

This chapter builds the foundation for your outline in a way that will make your book stand out from the others around it and pop-off the virtual shelves.

The Key Elements

Dave Chelsen, the Kindlepreneur,

experimented with just a few things, and proved that he could take the same book, change the title, the cover, and the book blurb, and shoot the sales of the book way up. He would change them back again and prove that the sales of the book fell off again. If you publish on Kindle first, you have the best chance of finding what works best for your book. You can experiment with a few different covers, titles, and book blurbs. When you have a combination that seems to work best, then you could publish to hard-copy with Amazon or with Createspace, where the title can't be changed. That gives you an eBook and a paperback!

Why do I bring these things up now, so early in the process? Because the most important part of starting your outline is having a really good topic and a great angle on that topic. I'll bet you are screaming in your head right now: "Wait a minute, you were just talking about a cover, title, and book blurb, where did this topic stuff come from?"

Well think about it. If you have the world's best cover, best title, and best book blurb, but the book is about a topic that no one has any interest in, will you sell any books? The answer is "NO." The topic will determine a lot about the cover, the title, and the book blurb. The topic is the catalyst for all of the marketing variables that make a difference for your book. You have to choose a GREAT topic for your book.

How to Choose a Topic

It is time to start a list of topics that you can choose from for your book.

1) Start your list with the things that you know.
Things at Work
a) What skills at work do you have that others would love to learn?
b) What do others at work come to you for?
c) What are you known for?
d) What are you the "go to" person for?
e) What did you study years to learn?
f) What problems can you solve?
g) How do you handle the problems as they come in?
h) How do you make your work environment better?
i) What would you change if you were in charge?

Hobbies and Leisure
a) What past times do you enjoy?
b) What sports or hobbies do you participate in?

c) What skills from those activities do you do well?

d) Which skills could you teach to others?

e) What advice would you give to beginners?

f) How would you coach the more advanced participants?

g) What does it take to get from beginner to advanced?

h) What awards or contests have you won?

i) What traditions or recipes can you pass on that you learned from you parents or grandparents?

Life lessons

a) What problems have you overcome in your life?

b) What problems have you helped family members or friends get through?

c) What hard lessons has life taught you?

d) What advice would you give to a teenager?

e) What life lessons have you learned from others that have impacted you, and why?

f) What would make your life or the lives of others around you better?

g) How have you dealt with difficult issues: depression, anxiety, stress, eating disorders, health problems, etc.?

The above list is not inclusive by any means. Write down your response to the most interesting questions above, and then think about any other questions that might interest other people about you. Write down your responses to those questions. You should have the beginnings of a nice list of possible topics to write about.

2) Make another list with the things that you like and are passionate about.

 a) What interests you in your life?

 b) What do you like to do with your free time?

 c) What would you do if you had the money and time to do it?

 d) What kinds of problems or puzzles do you like to solve?

 e) What kinds of books interest you?

 f) Where do you gravitate to in the library?

 g) What animals interest you?

 h) Where have you traveled to? What was different there?

 i) Where would you like to travel to and why?

 j) What kind of art or hobbies tickle your interests?

 k) What types of things help you relax and make you feel at home?

 l) What do you do for others?

m) What do you do for fun?
n) What do you do when you are bored?
o) What do you do when you are excited?

Actually, this list can and should continue far from this point. Just put down on paper the things that appeal to you. Don't censure any one of them at this time, just put them down on paper or in a Word document. Keep putting down the things that you like. Keep in mind that you can write a book about a subject that you LOVE even if you aren't an expert. People love to hear the story of the "journey." You can document what you did to learn about the subject and to experience it.

In the figure below, you can see an example of a journey book. It is taken from the table of contents of "Read my Hips" by Kimberly Brittingham.

The subject is about loving your body and getting away from body shaming. But the story is told about how she moved from feeling ashamed of her body to actually loving her body. This type of book could be made about learning a hobby or craft, about trying your hand at a job, or about how you learned to deal with one of life's difficult problems.

You can write about things that you love in this way, without trying to act like you are an expert. You are only inviting people to come on the learning journey with you and see what you experienced, what worked for you. You can tell about the things that didn't work for you and "debunk" the myths that are so popular with your particular journey.

Introduction: Read My Hips

PART ONE: DITCHING DIETING

Ring Dings
Glory Davis Made Me Believe in Total Transformation
Bacon-Cheddar Melt
We Were the Weight Loss Counselors
Can't Stand the Farm Stand
Belly

PART TWO: LOVING MY BODY

Strut
A Tale of Two Photo Sessions
My Grandmother: Forever in My Arms
Gym Dandies
Out on a Limb

PART THREE: LIVING LARGE

Boys Who Said Yes
Fat Aunt Phyllis
Fat Is Contagious
When the Avenue Walks on *You*
Video Star
Reach the Beach

Acknowledgments

Figure 5, Example Outline of a Journey Book

3) Make a list of topics that are popular.

How to choose a topic that is popular: (If you have ever heard the song "Popular" from the Broadway Hit "Wicked", then I want the tune to run through your head right now!) How can you tell if the topic is popular? Well, start with Google. Type in a few words of a possible topic in the search field of Google.

Do you see your search term in the dropdown suggestions? (as shown in Figure 1 below) If you do, then it has potential of being a popular topic. After hitting search, are there a good number of related results? The topic should have some traction on Google to show that it is interesting to people.

Figure 6, Google Drop Down Suggestions

A more relevant test, however is on Amazon. Amazon, in the end, is a search engine, a lot like Google, but people who search on Amazon are actually looking for something to BUY. Searchers on Google might just be looking for information. Those on Amazon have, at least, determined that they would like to see what is FOR SALE.

After looking on Amazon, try What's Trending on Twitter

(https://twitter.com/whatstrending?).

If you are on Facebook, on the right-hand side of your news feed is a "Trending" headline. That is a trending feed tailored just for you. YouTube has trending videos via the menu on the left of the home page. Google has a site called "Google Trends". The home page of Reddit is all about trending topics. Another site with popular social trends is BuzzSumo.

Popular AND Profitable

OK, so maybe you have found some ideas that seem to be popular, but are those topics actually profitable. If you were to write a book on one of those "trending" topics, would you actually be able to sell a few copies? Well, here you have to do a little bit of home work in the way of analyzing the topic. That can be done easily from Amazon.

Open up Amazon.com in your browser. Click on the drop down that says "All", now select Kindle Store as shown in the red circle in the figure below.

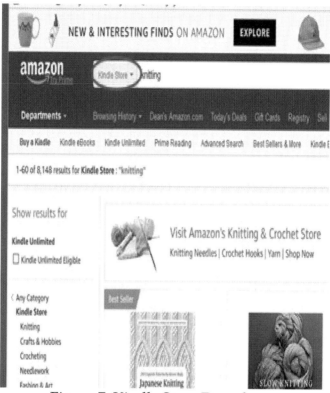

Figure 7, Kindle Store Dropdown

Start typing your topic into the Amazon search field. Again, look at the drop-down suggestions as shown in the figure below. Do many suggestions appear under the search field? If many appear, the topic might be popular on Amazon. If the suggestions seem relevant to your topic, click on the suggestions. Are there many relevant books that come up as a result of the search?

Are there any books that have the exact suggested phrase as the drop-down suggestion that you selected. If there is not a book title on the front page of the search results that has that exact phrase in it, then write down that phrase—using that phrase in the title might be a shortcut to getting your book found.

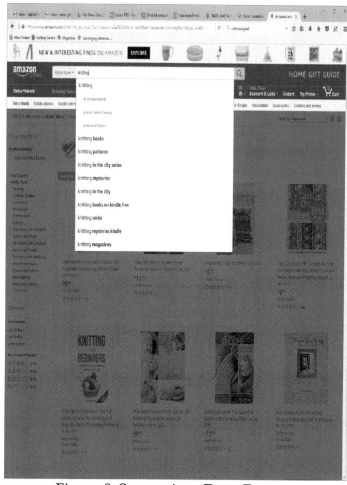

Figure 8, Suggestions Drop Down

Here is why: Amazon only stores suggestions many people have typed into the search field.

If there are a lot of people who have typed in a specific phrase looking for a book about that exact topic — then perhaps you should give them one! There are a lot of other factors to producing a book that sells, but never underestimate the value of a good title. Amazon uses the words and phrases in the title as the biggest weight in determining whether a book matches the search criteria of someone searching on their website. For nonfiction, determining a title may be the most important decision you can make. The title can also become a driving factor in helping you create your outline.

Expanding Your Base of Topic Ideas

You have a topic that you want to address in your book, but keep an open mind at this time as to what aspects you want to emphasize and what angle you want to write to. You may want to do a little more drop-down suggestion mining. Remember that the drop-down suggestions are actual phrases that customers have typed into Amazon looking for books about your topic. I find it useful to type in one keyword or short keyword phrase first.

For example, if my topic was about knitting, I would type in knitting in the search field of Amazon. I would see 10 suggestions below the search bar. Then I would add a space after the word knitting. Then I would add the letter a, so now I have "knitting a" in the search field of Amazon, and suddenly the 10 suggestions have changed to suggestions with knitting and words that start with the letter a.

You can repeat this with the letter b, then the letter c, etc. Capture the suggestions that pop out at you on paper or in a word processor or spreadsheet. The phrases that come up might give you great ideas for the main topic, subtopics, or even sideline things to address in your book. These phrases can be used as "keywords" that can be associated with your book when you publish it on Amazon.

There is a website called https://ubersuggest.io/ . You can type in a keyword and it will collect a HUGE BUNCH of suggestions from different search engines. Here you get a lot of those suggestions at one time with a lot less work — and the use of the website is free!

The Intersection of Knowledge and Passion
"Happiness is at the intersection of your passions and learning from great people." Scott Weiss

If you have two lists, one from your

knowledge and one from your passions, then there is only one more list to make. The list centered on what is popular. This new list may answer the question: If you publish this book does it have a good chance of selling some copies? There are never any guarantees, but there is kind of a rule of thumb. Ask yourself this question: Are there similar books that are selling on Amazon without there being too much competition? You want some books on the same topic out there to show that there is an interest in the market, but you don't want so many of them that your book has no chance of being on the first page of results returned by Amazon.

Unless you have your own list of customers to sell to, then you are going to need Amazon's help to sell your book. You need your book to be on the first page of results when people type in the search words or phrases that correspond to your topic. You know what many of those words or phrases are by looking at the drop-down suggestions.

Now it is time to dig a little further into the phrases that you want in your title. In the exercise above, we were just looking to see if there were other books that had something to do with your topic. Now that you have found those books, let's see how the books are doing sales wise.

Open up a browser on your computer

and go to www.Amazon.com. Type the title of your book or the phrase that you think might be good in your title to see what books come up in the search results. Click on the very first book on the results page.

Scroll down to the Product Details section of the book that looks like the picture in the figure below.

Product details

File Size: 163965 KB
Print Length: 160 pages
Publisher: Tuttle Publishing (October 10, 2017)
Publication Date: October 10, 2017
Sold by: Amazon Digital Services LLC
Language: English
ASIN: B06XFZ4NPC
Text-to-Speech: Enabled
X-Ray: Enabled
Word Wise: Not Enabled
Lending: Not Enabled
Screen Reader: Supported
Enhanced Typesetting: Enabled
Amazon Best Sellers Rank: #13,084 Paid in Kindle Store (See Top 100 Paid in Kindle Store)
    #1 in Kindle Store > Kindle eBooks > Arts & Photography > Graphic Design > Commercial > Fashion Design
    #2 in Kindle Store > Kindle eBooks > Arts & Photography > Fashion
    #2 in Kindle Store > Kindle eBooks > Crafts, Hobbies & Home > Crafts & Hobbies > Fashion

Figure 9, Product Details

Look at the Amazon Best Seller Rank. Here the line "13,084 Paid in Kindle Store" tells us that there are 13,083 books that are selling better than this one. This book is the 13,084th best-selling book by sales numbers on all of

Amazon's kindle books at this very moment. The order of these books is re-calculated hourly. You can think of the books in Amazon being lined up from the #1 selling book down to the least selling book estimated at about 3.4 million books (and growing daily).

Their top 100 best-selling books are displayed here: https://www.amazon.com/gp/bestsellers/digital-text/ref=pd_dp_ts_digital-text_1 . These books are #1 Paid in Kindle Store, #2 Paid in Kindle Store, #3 Paid in Kindle Store, etc. down to #100 Paid in Kindle Store. What this doesn't say, specifically, is how many books are selling for this particular title. There is a table posted on the http://www.theresaragan.com/salesrankingchart/ web site that estimates the sales of books using this best-selling ranking. The table looks like this:

Amazon Best Seller Rank 50,000 to 100,000 - **selling close to 1 book a day.**

Amazon Best Seller Rank 10,000 to 50,000 - **selling 5 to 15 books a day**.

Amazon Best Seller Rank 5,500 to 10,000 - **selling 15 to 25 books a day.**

Amazon Best Seller Rank 3,000 to 5,500 - **selling 25 to 70 books a day.**

Amazon Best Seller Rank 1,500 to 3,000 - **selling 70 to 100 books a day.**

Amazon Best Seller Rank 750 to 1,500 - **selling 100 to 120 books a day.**

Amazon Best Seller Rank 500 to 750 - **selling 120 to 175 books a day.**

Amazon Best Seller Rank 350 to 500 - **selling 175 to 200 books a day.**

Amazon Best Seller Rank 200 to 350 - **selling 200 to 300 books a day.**

Amazon Best Seller Rank 35 to 200 - **selling 300 to 1,000 books a day.**

Amazon Best Seller Rank 20 to 35 - **selling 1,000 to 2,000 books a day.**

Amazon Best Seller Rank of 5 to 20 - **selling 2,000 to 3,000 books a day.**

Amazon Best Seller Rank of 1 to 5 - **selling 3,000+ books a day.**

Books with a Best Seller Rank of under 30,000 sell a few books every day, and show that the topic is popular and is selling.

Filtering Your Results Based on Criteria

What you want to see on that page of Amazon Results is three to five books that have sales ranks below #30,000. But you don't want to see all of the books on the page have a sales rank of #30,000 and below. In fact, you want to see many books on that page of 20 books that have sales ranks of #100,000 to #300,000. This would let you know that your book has a chance of ending up on the first page of search results on Amazon.

There is no guarantee, of course, but the prospects are good for the book you want to write.

You may want to try some variations of the keywords that you are thinking about and run through this test with them also. Which phrase seems to have the best popularity without being too crowded to get your book into?

At some point you will just have to choose a phrase that you will craft a title from, and the point of view that you will take with your book. Again, these may be things that you have already decided on, but going through the exercise above will help you feel confident that you have a great idea, or perhaps it will let you know that you may not have something worth pursuing.

Conclusion

The best books come out of the intersection of what you know, what you like, and what is popular. The structure and course of your book will depend a lot on your purpose for writing. If you are writing a book for a number of reasons that don't really include making money by publishing your book, then many of the topics in this section aren't that important.

However, if you want to sell a few copies of your book, and you want Amazon's help selling them, then you have to do a few things to help Amazon.

To make your book sellable, you will want to carefully select a topic that is popular and profitable. You will want to experiment with possible titles and angles for your book that will help keep it up in the search results on Amazon. If you would like to explore finding a topic to write about in more detail you might consider looking at this book: "Discover Book Ideas", https://www.amazon.com/Discover-Book-Ideas-Writing-Bestsellers-ebook/dp/B00IODSNVI

Exercises

Do the exercises and practice what you learn so that this information stays with you and makes a HUGE difference to your book.

1. Create your list of things that you know. Don't short yourself, put it all down on the paper.
2. Create your list of things that you like, that you are passionate about.
3. Create the list of things that are popular.

a. Open up Google then start typing in your keyword or keyword phrase. Write down the suggestions for that keyword phrase.

b. Optional: Look at any trending topics on social media or other sites.

c. Open up Amazon then start typing in your keyword or keyword phrase. Write down the suggestions for that keyword phrase.

4. Analyze the keywords for popularity.

a. While still on the Amazon page type in what you think you might make the title of your book. Is there a book with that exact title?

b. Type in the suggestions that you captured earlier. Is there a book with an exact match keyword phrase? If not, that phrase may make a good title, seeing it in the suggestions means that people are typing that phrase into Amazon.

c. Evaluate the books that come back from the Amazon search. Are there three to five of them that have sales ranks below 30,000 (this shows that there are books in that market that are making daily sales).? Are there a number of books with sales ranks in the 150,000+ range (this shows that you aren't competing with 20 other books with below 20,000 sales rank)? If so there is probably a market for your book and it may have a chance to get on the first page of search results in Amazon.

5. Look for the intersections. Are there things that are on all three lists? Are there things that

are similar on more than one list? Things that are on all three lists are the sweet spot, and would make for a great outline and book.

Take some time to do the exercises before going on, it could make a big difference in getting your book and your outline off to a great start.

Chapter Three – A Giant Panorama

I have travelled to Seattle many times, I have visited the Space Needle, I have crossed a bridge getting to Seattle and a different one leaving the city, but it wasn't until I flew out of Seattle that I saw for the first time that it is basically an island with a few bridges connecting it to the surrounding land masses. Outlining a book can be a lot like that. You tend to be very familiar with the bits and pieces that make up the bulk of what you want to say or write, but it is sometimes impossible to visualize the entire thing until you have stepped far enough away from the little pieces to see the entire panorama.

This chapter deals with getting the bits and pieces into a form where they are visible and you are able to begin compiling and organizing into a cohesive whole. There are a number of methodologies for this process, and I continue to use several.

Each time I think that I have exactly the methodology that I like, it evolves, and I find myself merging one aspect of one methodology into another, adding or taking away something.

So, I vacillate between methods, and will

change methods on the fly when things begin to seem easier one way over the other.

I have found success with each of these methods. I hope that these methods enable your imagination and allow you to find something far superior to my methods that will work wonders for you. Writing, after all, is individual, and for it to work for you, you will have to try different things until one resonates with you, and you become more productive than you thought possible. I'm going to show you a few of the methods that I find the most useful.

The Splat Method

Inspiration comes to me in spurts and fits. I hate that sometimes my best ideas occur to me when I just want to turn over and get some sleep, or sometimes, even worse, when I am driving alone and have no way to record the ideas. I have found that it is better for me to get up and jot down the ideas while they are fresh on my mind, then it seems that the tension about the ideas is gone. I can then lay back down and fall right to sleep, I have deposited my ideas and I know that I will be able to work on them over the following days.

I have found that it pays for me to find a parking lot or a rest area where I can pull over and throw those pressing ideas on to paper. Then my mind can relax for the rest of the trip.

What's on Your List?

What really works for me is lists of ideas. Sometimes the ideas are related and flow into each other, but more often it is kind of like a grocery list. I want to talk about this, and this, and this. Oh, and I can't forget to mention this, and this, and this. (See the figure below). I like to create my list over several days so that the ideas have time to "mix" and mature.

I keep a small notebook or a pack of sticky notes in the car, on my dresser, at my desk, etc. I make sure to jot down ideas as they come to me. More often than not, I end up with a few repeats, or ideas that are mostly the same, that have to be merged into one as the list develops. But I am careful to just write things down, without analyzing how I will use them, or even if they are worth including. They are just my seed ideas that I want to consider as my ideas propagate and begin to fill out.

Example of a List of Ideas

1. Outlining a book
2. Makes writing faster
3. tools for outlining
   a. mind-map software
   b. sticky notes
   c. butcher paper
   d. 3x5 cards
   e. notebooks
   f. word processor
      1. lists
4. Types of non-fiction books
   a. biography
   b. academic
   c. guides/manuals
   d. journalism
   e. travelogues
   f. self-help
5. Discovering Topics
6. Structure of Outlines
   a. Depends on purposes and types.
   b. Topic – top line
   c. Subtopics
   d. Sub-subtopics
   e. Related information
   f. Needs three to ten sections.
   g. Needs to be related to topic and subtopic.
7. Examples of good outlines
8. Why are you writing the book?
9. Authors that use outlines
   a. Brandon Sanderson
   b. Orson Scott Card
10. Condense outline for table of contents
11. Outline makes writing linear
12. Brain dump
    a. Get it all on paper
    b. Keep a notebook nearby.
    c. Use response stimulus
13. Condensing Outline for Table of Contents
14. Research
    a. Title and keyword research

Figure 10, Example of Lists

My lists will span several sheets of paper. I have found that single sided sheets that can be pulled out of my notebook are the best for me, because I can literally cut the lines apart and paste them on a giant piece of butcher paper in my own version of a mind map.

When I have just a small notebook to work with, I will fill up both sides of the paper, without leaving any spaces, then later I will transfer the ideas, one at a time, to sticky notes which I can place on a giant sheet of butcher paper or large sketchpad sheets taped together.

Why do I need such a large background sheet of paper? So that I can see everything visually, and so that I can begin to organize it into a blended whole. I have thought that a large whiteboard might be a better medium for the backdrop to the little slips of paper, but I really don't have a place to keep a large white board, so I default to the butcher paper. As an added benefit, the butcher paper rolls up nicely and stores easily when I'm not using it.

Growing Lists

Taking a step back to my list of topics and subtopics, I first try to get it all down on paper. I make a list as the ideas and topics that I want to cover come to me. I try not to censure the ideas as they come to me nor even actually control the process, as I am putting the ideas on paper. When I hit a lull and I can't think of any more items to add to the list, then I usually take out a new piece of paper.

I look at the first item on the list. Does it remind of anything else that needs to be added? If so, I add that to a new list on the new blank piece of paper. Why do I put these on a new piece of paper? This might sound kind of strange, but I find If I'm adding to the list that I started on — I lose track of which item I'm on and I end up spending a lot of unproductive time looping through the lines looking for where I left off instead of just writing. If I have two separate pieces of paper, I can keep track of where I'm at with one hand or with a sticky note, or with something else so that my work is all linear and I don't get lost.

The lists begin to grow, and I find that I tend to start remembering things in groups and clusters.
The different aspects of the topic, the questions and issues about the topic, the problems and possible solutions to those problems about the topic start to manifest themselves on my growing lists.

Now that I have everything that I know and can pull out of my memory down into these lists, now is the time that I would turn to some research. I'll address how I do research and what I look for in the next chapter.

Grouping My Ideas

There are natural ways to group data. I look for things like problems and solutions, questions and answers, essential or optional. I look for natural breaks in the information. What someone needs to know, what they need to do, what information is foundational and what information has to be developed on top of that. I look for natural steps. I find that a lot of people are motivated by how-to information that can be broken down into step-by-step instructions.

Physical VS Digital

I often work with pen and paper first for a number of reasons. First, I can pack a small notebook with me most everywhere that I go. Second, I can keep a notebook by my bed, in the car, and tucked into little cubbies at home or at work. I can jot down ideas where ever they come to me. I find it harder to keep a computer around, or use the tiny little keyboard on my phone.

I know of people who speak into a microphone attached to their computer and/or phone, they create mp3 recordings which they can get transcribed or they can run through a program such as Dragon Speak Naturally.

They can complete a whole book as a series of recorded messages. I'm quite jealous of them. I tried to write some books that way, and found that sitting in front of a microphone is more intimidating that I had anticipated.

I found that if I were at home with the microphone on, my son would immediately be at the door disturbing my dictation session. I tried doing the recording while driving, which was way too distracting to keep on topic, and had way too much background noise to create good transcriptions. Not to mention, was more dangerous than I had anticipated, just concentrating on talking made me miss turn offs, and surely made me a worse driver. Needless to say, I don't recommend the dictate-while-driving approach.

So, I have reverted to the pen and paper. Third, there is something associated with writing on paper, pulling out the scissors, using paste to place the strips of paper somewhere. I like the feel, sound, and smell of the whole process. It sort-of makes it more like play than like work.

This is very individual. Some people like the physical, others feel very awkward using them. Go with what suits you. I like doing the physical things first, then moving to the digital. That just works for me.

Below are alternate methods for putting

your ideas down and beginning the process that leads to a great book outline.

The Snowflake Method

There is a saying that no two snowflakes are the same. It holds true for stories and books as well. The snowflake method is more organized than the splat method. It starts with a single topic or phrase and branches out one branch at a time. I will draw a single line away from the central topic, then write one of the known major subtopics. Around this subtopic, I would draw a line out to a sub-subtopic, or something that relates to the subtopic that I have just put down on the paper or in a mind-mapping software program. As soon as I have exhausted everything that

I believe relates to this subtopic, then I will draw a new line from the center topic to a new subtopic and fill that cluster out as much as I can thing. I will continue filling this out, as if I were forming a snowflake, with as many points as there are subtopics to address.

I always use the snowflake method when I am collaborating with other authors, and often if I have to teach the topic. Why do I use this method for collaboration or teaching? Because it is easy to fit into a digital mind-map. Using mind-mapping software makes the subtopics infinitely expandable and the file can be shared and added to as easily as attaching it to an email. It isn't as easy to collaborate on as a Google Doc or a Google sheet where many people can enter information into a document simultaneously, but it does make the document shareable and editable by other people.

The 3X5 Card Method

When I was in High School and college I used 3X5 cards to write my notes on and annotate my resources on. That method came with me when I started writing books. What I love about the 3X5 card method is that I can rearrange the order of the cards at will. I would usually start at the dollar store looking for a set of markers or colored pencils with the most colors that I could pick up very cheap. I would also look for 3X5 cards there. My initial investment would be under five dollars. I would write all of my notes with pen, but I would use a marker or colored pencil to color the top right corner.

I would use a different color for each sub-topic. I kept an index of the colors and the subtopics that each color went with, that way I could spread the cards out while I was writing, but still coalesce them into a neat pile and wrap a rubber-band around them when I wasn't writing.

The advantages of the 3X5 card system is

the ability to change the organization at will, and to surround my work area with the cards that I needed while I was writing. If I could see the card and didn't need to stop writing to access my resources and notes my writing was much more fluid and fast!

The drawback to the 3X5 card method, however, is that so many of my resources today are digital. I store URLs, copy quotes, clip pictures, and make my own digital images. None of those transfer to 3X5 cards. I know that I can just make a note to represent the digital resource, and that would let me use the 3X5 card method anyway—but I have found that I like digital resources such as Scrivener and/or Microsoft Word to put a lot of that in. I still have stacks of cards around, and will probably complete another book or two out of the cards that I have started in the past.

Mind Maps

There are several programs available, many of them are free. Here is a link to eight mind mapping software applications http://www.makeuseof.com/tag/8-free-mind-map-tools-best-use/. If this is something you might want to try, one of these might work for you.

Mind mapping software allows you to create a single central topic, then link the subtopics together. Most of these applications will allow you to link subtopics to lower subtopics, creating a hierarchical structure that lets you see the relationships between items in the map. I have used a program called Xmind in the past and found it very useful. I still prefer the paper and sticky note version, so I rarely pull out my mind mapping software. But this could work well for you.

Conclusion

Get your ideas down onto paper or into a digital document before starting your outline. The more possible topics and subtopics you get down, the more likely that you will see the patterns in the data and will begin to see how to organize your book. Try different methods such as lists, mind maps, 3X5 cards, or the snowflake method. One or more of these methods will make sense to you, and you will begin to see the organization of your data coming together.

Exercises

Stop now and start putting your ideas together. Just pick one of the methods listed above. If it seems clumsy to you after a bit, try a different method.

1. Get your ideas down on paper or in a digital document.

2. Look at your ideas and begin to organize them into groups.

Chapter Four – Reasonable Research That Will Make Your Book Pop

Do you know who you are writing your book for? Nonfiction books are primary for education and enlightenment. Entertainment type book typically fall in the fiction category. With this being said, it is important to know how your book is going to educate, enlighten, and enrich the lives of people who read it. You need to target your book at a certain group of people and try to solve their problems, fix their issues, or educate them about how they can make changes in their lives to have better lives. There are primarily five places that you should look for some really good ideas about who needs the information you have, what they need, and how to help that particular group of people. Those places are 1) websites, 2) forums, 3) Facebook groups, 4) courses and manuals, 5) other Amazon books.

What do you want to glean from these resources? 1) Find out about the people that need help with the topic such as 2)

What do they need? 3) Why are they having the problems that they have? 4) Why aren't common fixes working for them? 5) What are the common solutions for these problems? 6) What are the REAL pain-points? 7) What stops these people from getting the help that they need? 8) What can you offer them that is being missed by other sources? 9) How can you improve the effectiveness of the solutions that they might be trying? If your book can answer these questions, then it will likely deliver the kinds of education and information that the reader is looking for.

Demographics

I love to dream that everyone needs my books and will read them. The reality is that those that need this book are limited and this book will speak to a certain demographic SLIGHTLY better than others. How do you know what group that will be? Start with the demographic information.

According to DataUSA (https://datausa.io/profile/soc/273043/) Writers and Authors have an average age of about 42.6 years old. The diversity of this group is that 57.4% are female, and a slightly larger percentage of those are white by ethnicity.

Writers and Authors tend to have a little more education than non-writers, and their skill sets are extremely diverse. How does that help me? Well, now that I know what my AVERAGE reader might look like, I can make sure that I address issues that might be more important to that group more than others.

For example, if more of my readers are likely to be female, then, perhaps, I need to refer to the pronoun "she" more often. I should consider more feminine images on the cover. Perhaps I need to make sure there are more examples that use the experience of women in my writing. But, if my demographic shows that the average reader will be male, then I might want more sports stories in my examples, more logical appeal rather than emotional appeal. If my average reader is middle age, then perhaps I want to include the perspective of a parent with teenagers in the home. Whereas if the average reader of my book would typically be a millennial, then I might look at how my topic relates to what younger people might do — schooling, travel, dating, etc.

A book makes an impression on a person when they are able to relate to the author and to the experiences the author is sharing.

Some of those relating points will be purely around the topic itself, but many of the other life lessons that you as an author share will revolve around events in your own life.

Try to share more of the experiences around the demographics of your average reader. There will be more people who read your works that will be able to identify with you as an author first, then with what you have to say about your topic.

There is one thing I would like to mention at this point. As an author you can choose to write to a demographic that is outside the average for a specific topic. Why would you do this? Because you can let people know by the title what demographic it is for, and fill a "hole" in the market for that particular group. An example of this is Jack Canfield's "Chicken Soup for the Soul" series. Where each different title tells you who the book is written for, such as "Chicken Soup for the Teenage Soul" or "Chicken Soup for the Cancer Survivor's Soul."

Do you see how the title also talks directly to the exact demographics for the book and also pinpoints its market perfectly.

Some of the most successful non-fictions books have done just that, taken a VERY popular subject, then pinpointed a specific demographic.

This narrows the people that the book will interest, but increases the likelihood that those who read the book will "relate" to it and will LOVE the book. Narrowing and pinpointing a specific group of people will almost always be more successful than taking the broad approach because one set of your demographic or another will always not relate to the point of view that you are writing from, if you attempt to make your book generic and be for everyone!

Researching Your Topic on Websites

Google can be your friend. Type in your topic in the search field in Google and see what comes back in the results. I hope there are a number of good articles from websites related to your topic. You may want to make a quick list of a number of the most popular websites that show up in your search and the most popular stories on those websites. Websites about a topic show that there is a lot of interest in the topic. The most popular stories on that website usually showcase the most important issues for that topic. I will usually write down the title of the most popular articles on the top three to five websites that Google takes me to.

I try to stay away from websites that are accumulators for many subjects like news feeds or Ezine Articles, and concentrate on the websites that have one or more of the keywords for my topic in their name.

For example, let's say that I want to research digital photography. I will type digital photography into the search field of Google and get thousands of results. Among the first ones on the page is the website www.dpreview.com .

The dp is an acronym for Digital Photography. The keyword is in the name of the website — it is likely a topic website. So, I should go there for my research. The next one is www.dpmag.com . This one is Digital Photography Magazine. Again, my topic keyword is in the name of the site. This would also be a great resource.

I would look for issues and problems that jump off the page at me and I would write down the titles to those articles. I would start to put those issues and ideas into my brain dump of what I want to discuss in my book. These issues appear to be what is important to current people talking about the topic via web pages. It might be a good idea to include these types of trending issues in your book.

Researching Your Topic on Forums

When I'm at work and looking for someone to get information from, but I don't know exactly who to ask, I head for the water cooler or the break room.

Why? Because there will be someone there that I can ask and they will not be really busy with other things at the time and will at least be willing to discuss where to look for the answers that I need. If there were a digital "water cooler" built around specific topics, then that place would be forums. These are the places that people who are interested in a specific topic hang out to discuss it. Google can help you find these forums by typing in your keyword phrase in Google's search field, followed by the word forum. Find three or four in the search results that look interesting. Most forums will require a free registration, then you can read, search, or even participate in the discussions.

Forums can be set up by threads, categories, or even just the most recent discussions. Sometimes you can search on the number of people that have responded to or how many people have read a thread, other time you just have to go with the latest discussions on the page.

The idea, once you get on a forum, is to jot down ideas about what people are discussing.
These types of threads can be subtopics for your book.

Following the threads or discussions to their conclusion, there can be ideas about not just problems that people are running into currently, but also about the best solutions to problems.

I have spent some time on a few forums, and over time have added my own questions and used the answers from other readers as information that I could write into my books. Often authority figures in the topic will frequent the forums to answer questions and to keep up-to-date on the problems and issues surrounding the topic.

Researching Your Topic on Facebook Groups

Facebook allows you to join groups that regularly discuss specific topics. Login to Facebook, then in the search field type your keyword or keyword phrase then hit enter. A new bar will appear right under the search bar. On that bar select the "groups" button, as shown in the figure below.

Figure 11, Selection Bar to Choose Groups

Now you have a list of Facebook Groups that you can select from. You will have to join the group to read its contents. Search through a number of posts and write down the interesting ones. This should give you more information about what people find important about your topic.

Researching Your Topic from Courses

I love learning. I graduated from the University of Phoenix with a Master's Degree. The University of Phoenix was just starting to dabble in distance learning. I fell in love with the idea. I began taking courses that were held and distributed electronically. I am still taking courses on Udemy, a digital learning academy. If I want to learn a little bit about a subject, I will often buy or check out a book—but if I really need to learn it and understand it, I will take a course.

Udemy is a great resource for discovery of important issues about your topic. Go to www.udemy.com then type your keyword phrase in to the "Search for Courses" field. Look at the courses that come up in the results fields.

One of the things that I love about Udemy is the transparency about the courses. There is a "What Will I Learn" section that pitches the course, a section on what the course includes such as how many hours of video, a description of the course, a comparison with other similar courses, and a "Curriculum for This Course." You can even listen to the first two lessons as a Preview. I use the "Curriculum for This Course" as a table of contents for the course and look for subtopics that might be covered here that I haven't put into my notes or mind map.

Usually, at this point my mind map is bulging. I have many, many subtopics to discuss. The last resource, however, is the one that I use to set my book apart from the others.

Researching Your Topic with Other Amazon Books

You should have already looked at the covers and titles of the other books on Amazon about your topic. I would pick the most popular and the best-selling books that Amazon returns to you in their search results and I would look at 1) the table of contents. 2) some of the reviews. The table of contents for each book is often the outline for that book.

If you want to practice writing good outlines, simply type out each line of the table of contents of books on your topic found on Amazon. You will see how another author's book is organized, and what subtopics that author thought were important. Are you missing any of the subtopics that each book you look at has touched on? Jot those missing subtopics into your own mind-map.

When I first learned that I could publish my own books, I realized that the table of contents of other books on my topic were very valuable in showing how other people had organized their books. I would type out a table of contents and pretend to place my own content into the subtopics that other authors had created. I felt like this exercise helped me see patterns and organizations. Seeing this made it easier for me to look at the chaos of my own mind-map and start putting the subtopics together and putting my own content in those subtopics.

Don't steal anyone else's table of contents,

or even their specific layout, but think about their organization and see if you can use the influence of their organization to create an organization that is uniquely yours, but borrows a bit from the best layouts you run into. Most of all, make sure that you aren't missing any very important subtopics found in other books!

Finally, look at the reviews for other people's books on the topic. I like to browse through a number of the reviews, but I concentrate on the four-star and two-star reviews. Why? Because the five-star reviews tend to over-state the good of the book, and the one-star reviews tend to over-state the bad and/or are simply written by jealous and cranky people, and aren't worth reading.

What I want to find out is 1) what do people like about the book, and 2) what do people think is missing or could be better.

The reviews can tell you what you should do with your book, what the other book was missing, and what you definitely don't want to do with your book. This information is golden, and you can use it in your introduction.

"This book explains well how to do _____, that is missing in many popular books on this topic."

Conclusion

A little bit of research before you get very

far into creating your book outline can make your job much easier. Discovering what other people are writing about, looking at the table of contents and the reviews for other books on your topic can really help you discover meaningful subtopics that should be covered, what people are looking for in a book on that topic, and can even tell you what other authors have left out, or what they didn't cover well. All of these things can make your book a cut above everything else that is available on the Kindle market right now.

Exercises

1. Stop reading now and pull up some reasonable research. Open the table of contents on three to five other books on Amazon about your topic. Are there subtopics there that you might want to include in your book? Jot those subtopics down.
2. Now look at the reviews for those books. Specifically look at the four and two start reviews. What did the reviewers say that the author did well? What is missing or what did the reviewers feel the authors did not do well. Jot down those ideas as well.

Chapter Five – Types of Nonfiction Books and Examples of Outlines

This chapter is dedicated to examples of types of nonfiction books and outlines for those types of books. I hope these examples give you a great place to start as you are putting your outline together.

The How-To Book

I'm kind of a hands-on type of person. I like learning as I try to do things. I find that I don't even know the right questions to ask until I "get my hands dirty" by giving something a try. I bring this up because my favorite type of nonfiction book is the "How-To" book. When I search on Amazon for a How-To book, the first one to come up is Michael Bierut's "How To" (use graphic design to sell things, explain things, make things look better, make people laugh, make people cry, and every once in a while, change the world) https://www.amazon.com/How-Michael-Bierut-ebook/dp/B019MMUASI . I love the outline (table of contents) of this book! It uses "how to" in so many chapters: (as shown in the figure below)

Figure 12, Outline of a "How To" book

Almost every topic that you might want to teach to someone can be broken down into a number of "how-to" pieces. The books that have had the most impact on me have been how-to books. Usually, when I need to learn a skill, I find a how-to book.

The book gives step-by-step instructions about how to do exactly what I need to do. This type of book really speaks to me, so it is the first type of book that I want to analyze. Here is the outline for Guy Kawasaki and Shawn Welch's "APE: Author, Publisher, Entrepreneur—How to Publish a Book (shown in the figure below) https://www.amazon.com/APE-Author-Publisher-Entrepreneur-How-Publish-ebook/dp/B00AGFU5VS . I gleaned so much from this book!

6. How to Write Your Book
7. How to Finance Your Book
8. How to Edit Your Book
9. How to Avoid the Self-Published Look
10. How to Get an Effective Book Cover
11. Understanding Book Distribution
12. How to Sell Your Ebook Through Amazon, Apple, Barnes & Noble, Google, and Kobo
13. How to Convert Your File
14. How to Sell Ebooks Directly to Readers
15. How to Use Author-Services Companies
16. How to Use Print-on-Demand Companies
17. How to Upload Your Book
18. How to Price Your Book
19. How to Create Audio and Foreign Language Versions of Your Book
20. Self-Publishing Issues
21. How to Navigate Amazon
22. How to Guerrilla-Market Your Book
23. How to Build an Enchanting Personal Brand
24. How to Choose a Platform Tool
25. How to Create a Social-Media Profile
26. How to Share on Social Media
27. How to Comment and Respond on Social Media
28. How to Pitch Bloggers and Reviewers
29. How We APEd This Book

Figure 13, Outline of APE: Author, Publisher, Entrepreneur

Notice how most chapters start with How To! For very powerful nonfiction books follow this outline of your own topic. Make as many of the chapters into how-to sentences. You will be amazed at how powerful this approach is, and how easy writing the book becomes after you have identified the "how to" portions of the book.

The Step-by-Step book

A sub-section of the How-To books are the Step-by-Step books.

If you can take a single topic and narrow it down to a small number of repeatable steps, then you have a "recipe", so to speak, of how to do some particular thing. People love this direct, actionable approach. I used this approach to create one of the first books that I wrote. It was called "Write a Step-by-Step Book" (https://www.amazon.com/Write-Step-Step-Book-Bestsellers-ebook/dp/B00I0MKFVY) I found it to be very easy to put together. Just make sure all of the steps are there, and in the right order. Talk about how to do each step, and what results to expect as the step is complete.

Here are some great step-by-step book outlines:

10 Steps to Earning Awesome Grades, by Thomas Frank
https://www.amazon.com/Steps-Earning-Awesome-Grades-Studying-ebook

Table of Contents

Figure 14, Step-By-Step Book Outline

Notice how most chapters start with the step number. Writing this type of book flows so nicely. Step, by step, by step, until you reach your final destination!

Here is another type of book that features a step per day. Training Your Own Service Dog: Step by Step Instructions with 30-day Intensive Training Program to Get You Started by Lelah Sullivan and AKA Shana Cohen. https://www.amazon.com/dp/B015SJ32AM The partial outline is shown in the figure below.

Contents

Figure 15, Partial Outline of Step-by-Step Book With Daily Steps

Notice how each chapter is the step for the day. This type of book works well for books that are designed to change behavior. Here the change in behavior is geared towards a service dog, but most self-help books will have this type of outline with daily tasks that should become habits as the days go by.

Problem-Solution Books

These books might be a subset of the how-to books. Like how to lose weight or how to cure acne, but I feel like they can have a very different structure and outline. The Problem-Solution book has to catch a person's interest by empathy. Kind of a "you have this problem, I've had this problem, or I know of people who have had this problem, and there is a way to relieve your suffering."

Here is a good outline from Dean Sherzai and Ayesha Sherzai in their book "The Alzheimer's Solution." https://www.amazon.com/Alzheimers-Solution-Breakthrough-Symptoms-Cognitive-ebook/dp/B01N5PY7CU . See the figure below.

Dedication

Introduction

SECTION ONE: The Truth About Alzheimer's

SECTION TWO: The NEURO Plan

Figure 16, Outline of a Problem-Solution Book

Notice how the first section of the book is all about describing the problem, and in this case how people misunderstand the problem. A good problem-solution book always starts by connecting to the reader with stories or experiences about the problem and an explanation about why someone has to deal with the problem or do something about the problem instead of just letting it go.

The rest of the book is about how to solve the problem. This can include multiple things that should be done for the solution and/or multiple solutions. A good problem-solution book will have a conclusion and some very good actionable things that can easily and immediately be started on.

A special case of the problem-solution book is the "One Problem-One Solution" book. Many writers advocate this approach to writing a book fast. It works because it is very linear. There is only one problem to worry about and explaining how to solve that one problem. A good example of this type of a book outline can be found in the table of contents for Dennis Becker's book called "One Problem Writing." Shown in the figure below.
https://www.amazon.com/One-Problem-Writing-Writers-Speed-Writing-Non-Fiction-ebook/dp/B00PJ53404

About Me

Copyright

Join the IM Inside Track

1. Why Writing One-Problem, One-Solution Books Is An Amazing Way to Earn a Living

2. How Other Book Creation Courses Have Failed You

3. Why It's a Great Idea to Write Books

4. How to Find a Topic To Write About

5. How to Choose a Topic

6. Focusing On Your Topic

7. Ask Yourself Some Questions

8. Finding Sources for Research

9. Starting to Research

10. In-Depth Research

11. If You Know the Topic by Heart...

12. Sample Book Format

13. How to Stay on Topic

14. Be Prepared to Add Some Personality

Figure 17, Partial Outline for a One Problem-One Solution Book

The first part of this book focuses on the problem, then the following chapters are about how to solve the problem. A very straight-forward, linear way of writing a book, and a methodology that I would definitely recommend for a first or second book. These books will often be smaller than other books from three thousand words to about 10 thousand words. However, they can be very useful for readers—readers will feel like there is no fluff, if you can actually keep them focused to one problem one solution.

A Craft or Hobby Book

What crafts or hobbies do you enjoy? Would you recommend these crafts or hobbies to others? What was it like when you first started with this craft or hobby? Would you have liked to have had some help getting started or even just understanding the new vocabulary?

There are many craft and hobby books on Amazon. However, there is plenty of room for many more. Pinterest can be a good place to get ideas for projects that are popular with your craft or hobby.

A book about a craft or hobby will usually have some instructions, some tips and tricks, and usually one or more workable projects in the craft or hobby. Here is a good example of the outline for a Woodworking craft book. From the book "Woodworking: Woodworking Projects and Plans" by Jeff Wood. https://www.amazon.com/Woodworking-Projects-Plans-Beginners-WoodWorking-ebook/dp/B01F4I2SH0 (Shown in the figure below).

Figure 18, Partial Outline of a Craft Book

Sports Books

Lots of people love sports. There are so many angles that you can use to write a sports book. From teaching skills to beginners, to analyzing strategies, teams, or individual players. If it is a sport that you love to participate in you can include your own story about what interested you in the sport and what experiences made the sport enjoyable for you. There is room for sports books from beginners, and kind of a journey book, to sideline fans, who just enjoy watching the sport from the couch.

There are so many titles and angles for sports books that I can't show you a typical outline for one. Instead I am going to give you a few titles and if you are interested in this type of book, please take time to look at a number of books that might be similar to what you think you want to write about.

Books about the game of Football
Football: 2017 NFHS Football Rules Book
https://www.amazon.com/2017-NFHS-Football-Rules-Book-ebook/dp/B072JHD8MZ
Football for Dummies
https://www.amazon.com/Football-Dummies-Howie-Long-ebook/dp/B00SZ637GK
Al Davis: Behind the Raiders Shied
https://www.amazon.com/Al-Davis-Behind-Raiders-Shield-ebook/dp/B075BMMNZQ
Take Your Eye Off the Ball 2.0: How to Watch Football by knowing Where to Look
https://www.amazon.com/Take-Your-Eye-Off-

And the list goes on and on. Books about the sport, about the leagues, about the players, even about how to watch the game. Every sport has something like this. Sports are popular, and if you have a new angle on the sport there will probably be some kind of market.

Question-Answer Books

Every topic has its difficult and burning questions. There are many books that can be written around the questions that people might have or the questions that people often ask. These books can be easy to assemble, especially if you asked many of those very questions yourself, once some time ago, when you were new to the topic.

This type of book begins with an introduction, then each chapter can deal with a different question. Here is a good example of an outline from this type of book. This partial outline comes from "Answers to Questions You've Never Asked" by Joseph Pisenti.

Shown in the figure below.

INTRODUCTION: WHO AM I AND WHY DOES THIS BOOK EXIST?

CHAPTER ONE: WHY DO STRANGE BORDERS EXIST?

CHAPTER TWO: WHAT IF HISTORICAL EMPIRES WERE TO REUNITE TODAY?

CHAPTER THREE: HOW FAR AWAY CAN YOU GET FROM CERTAIN THINGS?

CHAPTER FOUR: HOW MANY COUNTRIES ARE THERE IN THE WORLD—
    NOBODY KNOWS!

CHAPTER FIVE: A TUTORIAL ON CREATING YOUR OWN COUNTRY

CHAPTER SIX: PRESIDENTS, POLITICS, AND THE NUCLEAR FOOTBALL

CHAPTER SEVEN: WHY IS MONEY BACKED BY GOLD?

CHAPTER EIGHT: WHAT IS CREDIT AND WHERE DID IT COME FROM?

CHAPTER NINE: WHAT IS THE MOST DANGEROUS ROAD IN THE WORLD?

CHAPTER TEN: CAN YOU TURN THE EARTH INTO A SANDWICH?

Figure 19, Partial Outline of Question and
Answer Book

Questions can be the start to every
chapter of your book, and it will be interesting, if
you are answering the questions and asking
good questions. People are curious, and

questions can whet the appetite for answers.

The Interview Book

A subset of the question-answer book is the interview book. Sometimes you are able to get an expert to talk to you about a subject, and you are able to record the interview. The interview book is a transcript of that interview. This type of a book will generally have an introduction to the topic and an amazing introduction to the expert being interviewed.

The rest of the body of the book will be about the questions asked and how the expert answered those questions. Usually a conclusion will include how to learn more about the subject including how to contact the expert, and sometimes how to follow-up with getting on your email list or something to that effect.

You can transcribe the interview yourself or find someone on Fiverr.com or oDesk.com who will do the transcription based on the length of the video or recording or the word count.

This type of book can be completed

quickly because it mostly contains the transcription of the interview. Here is a great book outline that is representative of an interview book. The book "Positively Influential" by Rob Christensen (https://www.amazon.com/Positively-Influential-Professional-Networking-Attraction-ebook/dp/B0044KM262) has more than just one interview, it has several. See the Outline in the form of a table of contents below.

Table of Contents

Figure 20, Outline of an Interview book

Beginner Books and For Dummy's Books

Many people pick up a book because they want to start learning something that they have never done before, or have tried once and were not successful. There are many people who really need just the basics. The beauty of this market is that you don't have to be an expert to write this type of book, you just have to have a little more knowledge than those you are writing for, you will also need some patients to talk about the foundations and the details, and lots of enthusiasm for the topic.

Here is an example of a partial outline of a beginner's book. This book, "The Art of Crochet for Beginners" by Katrina Gale. https://www.amazon.com/Art-Crochet-Beginners-Visual-Guide-ebook/dp/B0772DF45X

Figure 21, Partial Outline for a Beginner's Book

As you can see the book will usually start out with an explanation of equipment and details about the basics of the topic. With those set up, go ahead and teach some steps and methods, but keep it simple! Save the complicated stuff for the advanced version.

There is a set of books going around that have become pretty popular. It is the "For Dummies" books. These types of books are simply beginner's books with plenty of pictures and simple steps. You can always expand with an advanced book if the beginner's book does well.

Advanced Books

Beginning books normally have a larger market, but are much harder to pinpoint the exact customer. Beginning books will appeal to people who have no experience at all with a topic to those who understand it pretty well, but just want to know more about it. Beginning books are hard to gage when it comes to knowing where each customer is in their current knowledge and how basic the content in that book actually needs to be.

Advanced books, however, must assume that readers have a basic knowledge and that they will understand some of the terminology of the industry. Advanced books can pinpoint their target readers much better, and can be easier to write from that perspective. The other advantage of advanced books is that there are fewer other books on the shelf, that means a lot less competition. In the figure below are some excerpts from outline of the book "Advanced Practice Nursing" by Susan M. DeNisco and Anne M. Barker.

Figure 22, Partial Outline of an Advance Book

What I want to point out is that chapter and section headings have the word advanced in them, letting people know that these are not basic topics. Advanced topics should be the more complex topics, or the ones that must be built on top of the fundamental principles that would normally be taught in a beginning book. Use wording such as "taking it to the next level", "building on earlier concepts", "after applying the basics", and "exploring further."

Readers, and would be readers, will be

able to see at a glance that these are non-basic or more complicated principles and concepts.

Expository Books

Expository books are those that try to open up the perspective of the reader and show them what they have been missing. They will try to explain the unexplainable. What, why, how, when might start the titles of these kind of books. They will often be about the biggest controversies of the moment.

The beauty of this type of book is that, at least while the issues are hot, they can be very hot sellers, and there are usually a lot of news articles and "talking heads" (chat shows on tv that are talking about the issue, person, or situation). With this type of book, an author will state an opinion and attempt to prove the opinion, or simply expose things that the reader can think about. If you have a political, religious, environmental, social, economic, or other types of opinion, this is the type of book for you.

These can usually be very fast to get to market, because you will know so much about the issue or concern, or there will be so much current information to research through. About the only requirement is that you have an opinion and that you state the opinion throughout the book.

In the figure below is a partial example of an outline of an expository book. This comes from "What Happened to Goldman Sachs:" by Steven Mandis.

Contents

Figure 23, Partial Outline of and Expository Book

If you look at the first chapter, you see that the author states his opinion, or at least an attempt at an opinion with "What Happened", then he continues to expose the details that make up justifying the opinion. Exposition books kind of follow that model.

Memoirs book

A memoirs book is a book that centers around events, celebrities, cultures, cults, and other sensational situations. If you look at the figure below you will see that the category is loaded with bestsellers. They answer the deep questions of what is it like to know Hillary Clinton or Warren Buffet? What was it like to survive the natural disasters of Hurricane Katrina or the tsunami in Japan? What could be told about the banking disaster of 2007, perhaps from a bank employee or someone close to the situation. What was it like to be a survivor of 911, or what was it like to lose a loved one there?

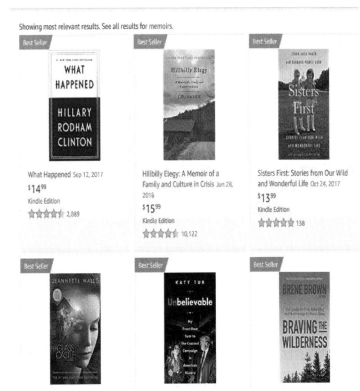

Figure 24, List of Bestsellers in the category of memoirs

Memoirs usually take on an emotional appeal. What was it like? How was it handled? And perhaps even What can be done? Memoirs can be kind of expository and/or sensational. People who like memoirs tend to look for the big reveals. If your life feels a bit like a soap-opera, or if it used to, then you might think about writing a memoirs book.

But because memoirs are about so many different things and are written for so many different reasons, there is no real standard outline. Looking at the table of contents of a number of memoirs and reading some might be your best way of preparing to write this type of nonfiction book.

Conclusion

There are a number of types of nonfictions books. This chapter displayed a number of examples of book outlines, mostly one or more for each type of book.

Exercises

1. Look over the 10 types of books discussed above.
2. Select a type of book and begin organizing your notes into groups.
3. You can start your outline now, or use one of the templates below.

Chapter Six – Book Outline Templates

This chapter contains a number of templates. You can use the templates as they are—cut and paste, then start filling in the information for your book, or just use the template as a model to follow. There really is no right or wrong way to do an outline. The important part is to just start on it.

T1 – How-to Book Outline Template

Front Matter (about the author, copywrite, publishing info)
Title
Subtitle

Introduction to main topic
       Benefits of learning how-to.
       What the book will do for the reader.
       (Maybe how the book is organized)

Chapter 1 Subtopic 1

Chapters can consist of different aspects of the topic or about separate projects.

Include things like specific instructions.

Include lots of examples and maybe even exercises.

Chapter 2 Subtopic 2

Chapter 3 Subtopic 3

.

.

.

Chapter N Subtopic N

Conclusion

T2 – Outline Template for Step-by-Step Books

Front Matter (about the author, copywrite, publishing info)

Title

Subtitle

Introduction to Topic or Project

Chapter 1 Step 1

Chapter 2 Step 2
Chapter 3 Step 3

.

.

.

Or an alternate to this is simple steps to each separate project.
Chapter 1 Project 1
    Step 1
    Step 2
    Step 3

    .

    .

    .

Chapter 2 Project 2
Chapter 3 Project 3

.

.

.

Chapter N Project N

Conclusion

T3 – Problem-Solution Book Outline Template

Front Matter (about the author, copywrite, publishing info)
Title
Subtitle

Introduction to the topic

Chapter 1 Problem Analysis
       Disadvantages of the problem.
       How bad things can get.
       What happens if the problem isn't solved.
       Why you really need a solution.
Chapter 2 Common myths about the problem.
Chapter 3 Why current solutions don't work
Chapter 4 Problem Solution # 1
Chapter 5 Problem Solution # 2

    .
    .
    .

Chapter N Problem Solution # N

Conclusion

T4 – Craft or Hobby Book Outline Template

Front Matter (about the author, copywrite, publishing info)
Title

Subtitle

Introduction to the craft or hobby

Chapter 1 Introduction to Projects
        Build excitement for the craft or hobby here.
        Things that you can do with the craft or hobby.
        Examples of crafts or activities that can be done.
Chapter 2 Introduction to tools and methodologies
        Tools needed for the craft.
        How to use the tools and other possible resources.
        Foundational principles for working the craft or hobby.
Chapter 3 Subtopic 1
        Any other foundational materials that need to be shared before getting into the projects.
        Subtopic 2
        Subtopic 3
        .
        .
        .
Chapter 4 Project 1
        Steps, examples, pictures, instructions, etc.
Chapter 5 Project 2

Chapter 6 Project 3

.

.

.

Chapter N Project N

Conclusion

T5 – Sports Book Outline Template

Front Matter (about the author, copywrite, publishing info)
Title
Subtitle

Introduction to the sport, athlete, team, or other aspect of a sport

Chapter 1 Foundational Information
        This can vary. Information about the sport, perhaps some history, what to watch for, important athletes in the sport and important teams, how the sport relates to countries and cultures, etc.
Chapter 2 Subtopic 1
Chapter 3 Subtopic 2

.
.
.

Chapter N Subtopic N
Conclusion

T6 – Question-Answer Book Outline Template

Front Matter (about the author, copywrite, publishing info)
Title
Subtitle

Introduction to the topic that the questions are clustered around

Chapter 1 Question 1 Answer 1
Chapter 2 Question 2 Answer 2
Chapter 3 Question 3 Answer 3
.
.
.

Alternately questions and answers can be grouped into pockets of related information

Chapter 1 Questions About Subtopic 1
    Question 1 Answer 1
    Question 2 Answer 2
    Question 3 Answer 3
Chapter 2 Questions About Subtopic 2
    Question 4 Answer 4
    Question 5 Answer 5
    Question 6 Answer 6
Chapter 3 Questions About Subtopic 3
    .
    .
    .
Chapter N Questions About Subtopic N

Conclusion
    Which questions should keep the reader thinking, how to do something with the information presented.

T7 – Interview Book Outline Template

Front Matter (about the author, copywrite, publishing info)
Title
Subtitle

Introduction
     Introduction to the topic and explanation that the book is based on an interview with some person or group that has something to do with your topic

Chapter 1 Who is the interview with and why should you read about it
     Information about the person or persons being interviewed.
     Information about the accomplishments, groups, certifications, etc. of the persons being interviewed.
     Why the information being presented is important.
Chapter 2 Subtopic 1
     Transcription from verbal or email interview
Chapter 3 Subtopic 2
     Transcription from verbal or email interview
Chapter 4 Subtopic 4

     .

     .

     .

Chapter N Subtopic N

Conclusion

Why this information is vital and how to apply it to the reader.

T8 – Beginner Books or For Dummies Book Outline Template

Front Matter (about the author, copywrite, publishing info)
Title
Subtitle

Introduction

Introduction to the topic

Chapter 1 Book made for Beginners

Why this book is for beginners.

Which topics are covered and which topics are left for the advanced learners

What readers will get from the book.

Chapter 2 Subtopic 1

Foundational principles.

What the reader will need to know, some definitions, some examples.

Chapter 3 Subtopic 2
Chapter 4 Subtopic 3
Chapter 5 Subtopic 4

.
.

Chapter N Subtopic N

Conclusion
    Summarize what the reader should have learned and how the reader can apply the learning.

T9 – Advanced Books Outline Template

Front Matter (about the author, copywrite, publishing info)
Title
Subtitle

Introduction
    Introduction to the topic

Chapter 1 Book Targeted to Advanced Participants
    Why this book was created and what readers should expect.
    Which topics are covered in this book and

which topics are better pursued in a beginning book.

What advanced participants should be able to do with the information in the book.
Chapter 2 Subtopic 1
Chapter 3 Subtopic 2
Chapter 4 Subtopic 3
Chapter 5 Subtopic 4

.

.

.

Chapter N Subtopic N

Conclusion

Summary of advanced topics covered. What readers should have gotten out of the book. Where to look if participants actually need to go back and read a beginning book.

T10 – Expository Books Outline Template

Front Matter (about the author, copywrite,

publishing info)
Title
Subtitle

Introduction
      Introduction to the issue or hot topic.

Chapter 1 Foundational Information
      History of the problem.
      Why it is a problem today.
      Who is involved in perpetuating the
problem.
      State the opinion that you are going to try
to prove or persuade people to accept.
Chapter 2 Subtopic 1
Chapter 3 Subtopic 2
Chapter 4 Subtopic 3
Chapter 5 Subtopic 4
      .

      .

      .

Chapter N Subtopic N

Alternately these chapters can be aimed at
people or groups involved.

Chapter 2 Group 1
Chapter 3 Group 2
Chapter 4 Group 3
      .

      .

.

Chapter N Subtopic N

Or the chapters can be aimed at events that
effected the problem

Chapter 2 Event 1
Chapter 3 Event 2
Chapter 4 Event 3

.

.

.

Chapter N Event N

Conclusion

Exposition books are based on an opinion.
Restate the opinion and what people should do
or think about the issue or hot topic.

No Book Template for Memoirs. They
take many forms. The best advice I can give is to
go to Amazon and look at several Table of
Contents for the top memoirs books. Read a few
of the memoirs books to understand what
people actually expect out of a memoirs book.

Conclusion from the Template Chapter

Above are 10 templates that you can use—cut and paste, then start filling in the template. Or you can just use the templates as a model, see what the structure is like, and try to put your own outline together with it.

Exercises

1. Just do it. Start your outline now.
2. Set a deadline for when your outline will be done.
3. Set aside time every day to write and start writing your book now!

I hope you have enjoyed the book.

If you have, please leave a review.

You can leave a review here: http://amzn.to/2Gg6Vzu

Reviews are so important to independent authors.

If notice any problems with the book, or you have any feedback on the book, please send it to me dgiles63@gmail.com. I answer all email.

Thank you for your purchase! It is very much appreciated.

Other Books by This Author

http://amzn.to/1WHw2Qo

http://amzn.to/1UiVtSu

http://amzn.to/1HXOyHm

https://www.amazon.com/dp/B00O9LIBMK

On the Lighter Side

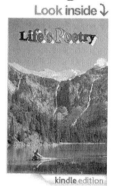

http://amzn.to/1KSZfgv

http://amzn.to/1UbXlSn

https://www.amazon.com/dp/B00DZVYG4W

https://www.amazon.com/dp/B00E45ADKE

Do you Like Coloring Books?

Check these out:

Relaxing Mandalas http://amzn.to/2eR50Tw
Funny Kids http://amzn.to/2dKdaMB
Twisted Mandalas http://amzn.to/2eRuOjK
Halloween Mandalas http://amzn.to/2f14upz
Thanksgiving Mandalas
http://amzn.to/2fPLsnR
Mindful Shapes http://amzn.to/2frWHAz
Christmas http://amzn.to/2gzdgIz
Relaxing Animals http://amzn.to/2gBY3I0
gift-page http://bit.ly/2eDcOcu

Resources

"Write. Publish. Repeat." By Sean Platt, Johnny
B. Truant, and David Write.
https://www.amazon.com/Publish-Repeat-No-
Luck-Required-Self-Publishing-Success-
ebook/dp/B00H26IFJS
"Author, Publisher, Entrepreneur" by Guy

Kawasaki, Shawn Welch
https://www.amazon.com/APE-Author-
Publisher-Entrepreneur-How-Publish-
ebook/dp/B00AGFU5VS
"On Writing" by Stephen King.
https://www.amazon.com/Writing-Memoir-
Craft-Stephen-King-ebook/dp/B000FC0SIM
"How to Write Science Fiction and Fantasy" by
Orson Scott Card.
https://www.amazon.com/Write-Science-
Fiction-Fantasy-Writing/dp/0898794161
"How I sold 80,000 Books: Book marketing for
Authors" by Alinka Rutkowska.
https://www.amazon.com/How-Sold-000-
Books-Publishing/dp/1943386056
"Steal Like an Artist" by Austin Kleon.
https://www.amazon.com/Steal-Like-Artist-
Things-Creative/dp/0761169253
"One Problem Writing" by Dennis Becker.
https://www.amazon.com/One-Problem-
Writing-Writers-Speed-Writing-Non-Fiction-
ebook/dp/B00PJ53404
"Outline to Finish Line" by Shelly Hitz.
https://www.amazon.com/Write-Book-Outline-
Finish-Line-ebook/dp/B00YJXXCQS
"How to Write a Book That's Complete" by Ian
Stables and Darek Doepker.
https://www.amazon.com/Write-Thats-
Complete-step-step-ebook/dp/B00D5FK80E

70715647R00069

Made in the USA
San Bernardino, CA
05 March 2018